D1607306

GRAPHIC DINOSAURS

ARCHAEOPTERYX

THE FIRST BIRD

ILLUSTRATED BY TERRY RILEY,
ROB SHONE, JAMIE WEST

PowerKiDS
press.

New York

Published in 2012 by The Rosen Publishing Group, Inc.
29 East 21st Street, New York, NY 10010

Designed and produced by
David West Books

Designed and written by Rob Shone

Photographic credits: 5t, Lip Kee; 5m, T. Voekler; 5b, Bird Brian; 30l–30m, H. Raab; 30r, Dinoguy.

Library of Congress Cataloging-in-Publication Data
Shone, Rob.
Archaeopteryx : the first bird / by Rob Shone.
p. cm. — (Graphic dinosaurs)
Includes index.
ISBN 978-1-4488-5204-8 (library binding) — ISBN 978-1-4488-5246-8 (pbk.) —
ISBN 978-1-4488-5247-5 (6-pack)
1. Archaeopteryx—Juvenile literature. I. Title.
QE872.A8S56 2012
568'.22—dc22
2010050996

Manufactured in China

CPSIA Compliance Information: Batch #DS1102PK:
For Further Information contact Rosen Publishing, New York, New York at 1-800-237-9932

CONTENTS

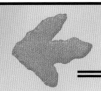 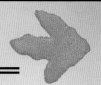

WHAT IS AN ARCHAEOPTERYX?

ARCHAEOPTERYX MEANS "ANCIENT WING."

Archaeopteryx had a long feathered tail that helped keep it balanced when it flew.

Archaeopteryx had good eyesight and a good sense of balance to help it fly through the forest.

Archaeopteryx had broad wings that were well suited for gliding flight.

Instead of a beak, Archaeopteryx had a snout filled with small sharp teeth.

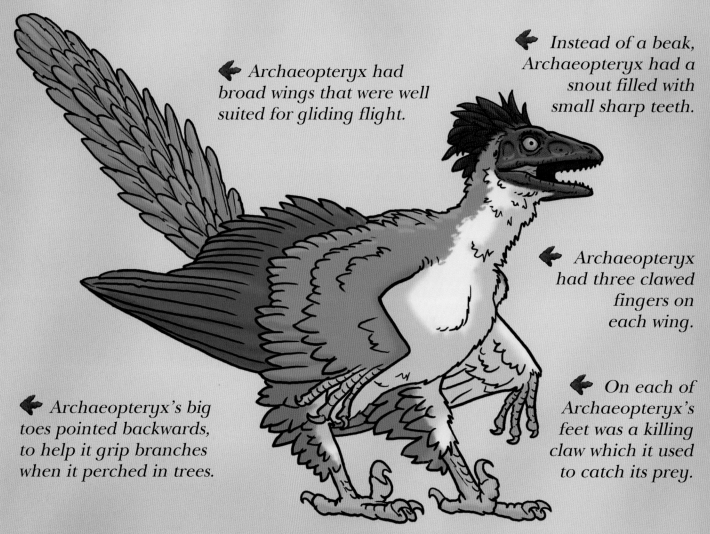

Archaeopteryx had three clawed fingers on each wing.

Archaeopteryx's big toes pointed backwards, to help it grip branches when it perched in trees.

On each of Archaeopteryx's feet was a killing claw which it used to catch its prey.

ARCHAEOPTERYX WAS A BIRD THAT LIVED AROUND 150 MILLION TO 145 MILLION YEARS AGO, DURING THE JURASSIC PERIOD. FOSSILS OF ITS SKELETON HAVE BEEN FOUND IN GERMANY.

An adult Archaeopteryx measured up to 20 inches (50 cm) in length, had a 2-foot (60-cm) wingspan, and weighed 9 ounces (250 gm).

BIRD OR DINOSAUR?

Most scientists think that Archaeopteryx was a bird. It had feathered wings and feet that allowed it to perch like modern birds. It had the good eyesight and sense of balance that birds need to fly, and many parts of its skeleton are similar to present-day birds. It was also very dinosaur like. It had teeth, a long bony tail, hand claws, and a killing claw on each foot. These features are all found on small meat-eating dinosaurs. Scientists believe that Archaeopteryx is the link that shows how birds **evolved** from dinosaurs.

The colugo (right) is a mammal that lives in the rain forests of Asia. Skin flaps that stretch between its wrists and ankles act like wings, allowing it to glide from tree to tree.

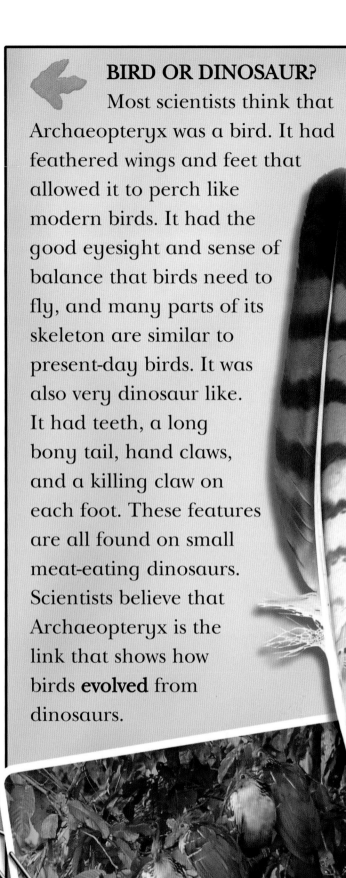

Archaeopteryx's wing feathers were very similar to the flight feathers of modern birds (left).

FLAP OR GLIDE?

Although it had feathered wings, Archaeopteryx probably did not fly by flapping them as modern birds do. Its chest muscles were not strong enough. It could have used its wings to glide, like a paper plane. It would have used its claws to climb up a tree and then glide above the forest floor to land on the trunk of a nearby tree.

The chicks of the South American hoatzin (left) have claws on their wings. They use them to climb through the branches of their tree home.

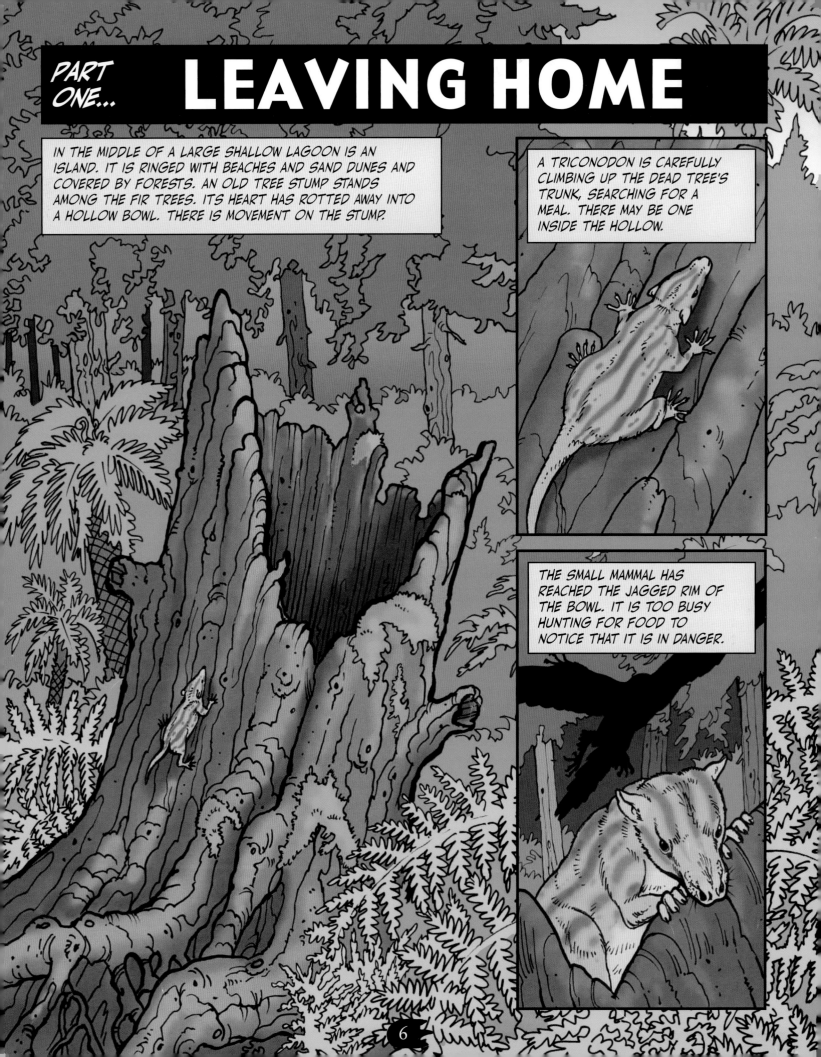

PART ONE... LEAVING HOME

IN THE MIDDLE OF A LARGE SHALLOW LAGOON IS AN ISLAND. IT IS RINGED WITH BEACHES AND SAND DUNES AND COVERED BY FORESTS. AN OLD TREE STUMP STANDS AMONG THE FIR TREES. ITS HEART HAS ROTTED AWAY INTO A HOLLOW BOWL. THERE IS MOVEMENT ON THE STUMP.

A TRICONODON IS CAREFULLY CLIMBING UP THE DEAD TREE'S TRUNK, SEARCHING FOR A MEAL. THERE MAY BE ONE INSIDE THE HOLLOW.

THE SMALL MAMMAL HAS REACHED THE JAGGED RIM OF THE BOWL. IT IS TOO BUSY HUNTING FOR FOOD TO NOTICE THAT IT IS IN DANGER.

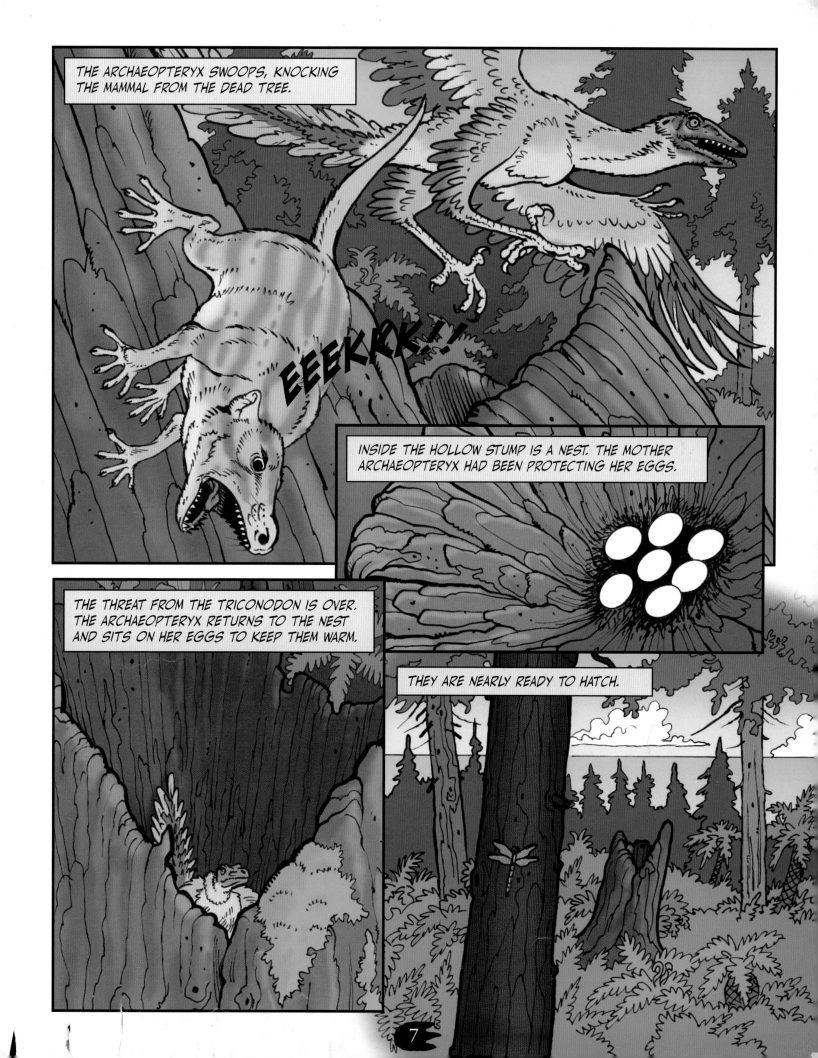

THE ARCHAEOPTERYX SWOOPS, KNOCKING THE MAMMAL FROM THE DEAD TREE.

EEEKKK!!!

INSIDE THE HOLLOW STUMP IS A NEST. THE MOTHER ARCHAEOPTERYX HAD BEEN PROTECTING HER EGGS.

THE THREAT FROM THE TRICONODON IS OVER. THE ARCHAEOPTERYX RETURNS TO THE NEST AND SITS ON HER EGGS TO KEEP THEM WARM.

THEY ARE NEARLY READY TO HATCH.

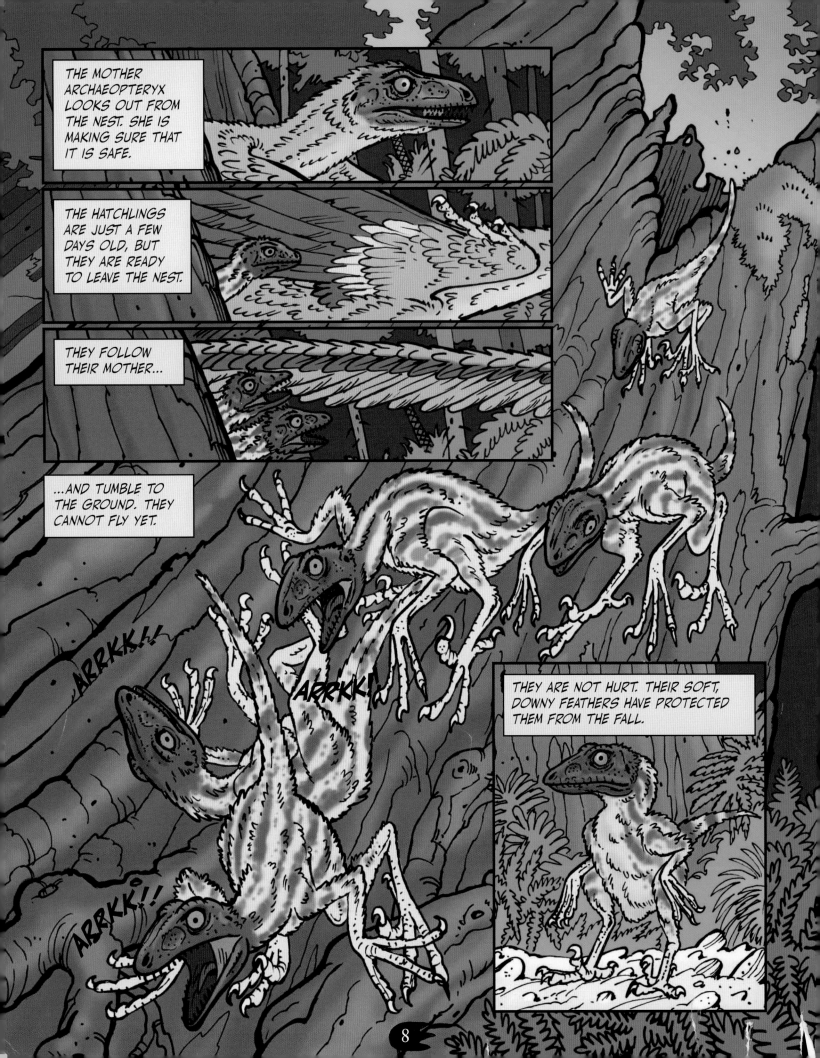

THE MOTHER ARCHAEOPTERYX LOOKS OUT FROM THE NEST. SHE IS MAKING SURE THAT IT IS SAFE.

THE HATCHLINGS ARE JUST A FEW DAYS OLD, BUT THEY ARE READY TO LEAVE THE NEST.

THEY FOLLOW THEIR MOTHER...

...AND TUMBLE TO THE GROUND. THEY CANNOT FLY YET.

ARRKK!!

ARRKK!

ARRKK!!

THEY ARE NOT HURT. THEIR SOFT, DOWNY FEATHERS HAVE PROTECTED THEM FROM THE FALL.

FOR THE FIRST FEW WEEKS THE HATCHLINGS STAY CLOSE TO THEIR MOTHER. THEY LEARN ALL THEY CAN FROM HER...

...AND RUN TO HER WHEN THERE IS DANGER.

WAARRKKK!!

AKK! AKK!

A HERD OF CAMPTOSAURUSES HAS WANDERED TOO CLOSE TO THE HATCHLINGS.

THE CAMPTOSAURUSES ARE PLANT-EATERS AND ARE NOT A THREAT TO THE TINY HATCHLINGS. EVEN SO, THEIR MOTHER BRAVELY PROTECTS THEM WHILE THE LARGE DINOSAURS PASS BY.

ARKK! ARKK!

ONCE THE HATCHLINGS ARE OLD ENOUGH TO LOOK AFTER THEMSELVES, THE MOTHER LEAVES.

THE HATCHLINGS SOON FIND THAT NOT ALL DINOSAURS ARE AS HARMLESS AS THE CAMPTOSAURUSES. THEY ARE BEING WATCHED.

A GROUP OF JURAVENATORS RUSH FROM THE UNDERGROWTH. THESE SMALL MEAT EATERS ARE NOT MUCH BIGGER THAN THE HATCHLINGS, BUT THEY ARE DEADLY HUNTERS.

SHAARRRGHH!!

THE HATCHLINGS RUN TO THE NEAREST TREE.

EACH FOOT HAS A HOOKED KILLING CLAW. THE HATCHLINGS USE THEM, AND THEIR WING CLAWS, TO **CLAMBER** TO SAFETY.

ONE OF THE HATCHLINGS IS TOO SLOW. IT DOES NOT REACH THE TREE IN TIME.

AARRRKK!!

SOON THE HATCHLINGS WILL BE TOO BIG FOR THE JURAVENATORS TO ATTACK. FOR NOW THEY WATCH AS THE LITTLE KILLERS FEED.

PART TWO... A FLYING LESSON

THE ARCHAEOPTERYX HATCHLING WATCHES AS THE BAVARISAURUS RUNS TOWARD THE TREE. HE HAS WAITED PATIENTLY FOR THIS MOMENT. AS SOON AS THE SMALL LIZARD IS CLOSE ENOUGH, HE WILL DROP FROM HIS PERCH AND STRIKE.

IT HAS BEEN SIX MONTHS SINCE HE LEFT THE NEST. HIS BROTHERS AND SISTERS ARE SCATTERED THROUGHOUT THE FOREST. HIS SOFT, DOWNY FEATHERS ARE FALLING OUT, AND LONG FLYING FEATHERS ARE GROWING IN THEIR PLACE.

THE LIZARD SCAMPERS RIGHT UNDER THE ARCHAEOPTERYX. HE OPENS HIS WINGS AND LETS GO OF HIS PERCH.

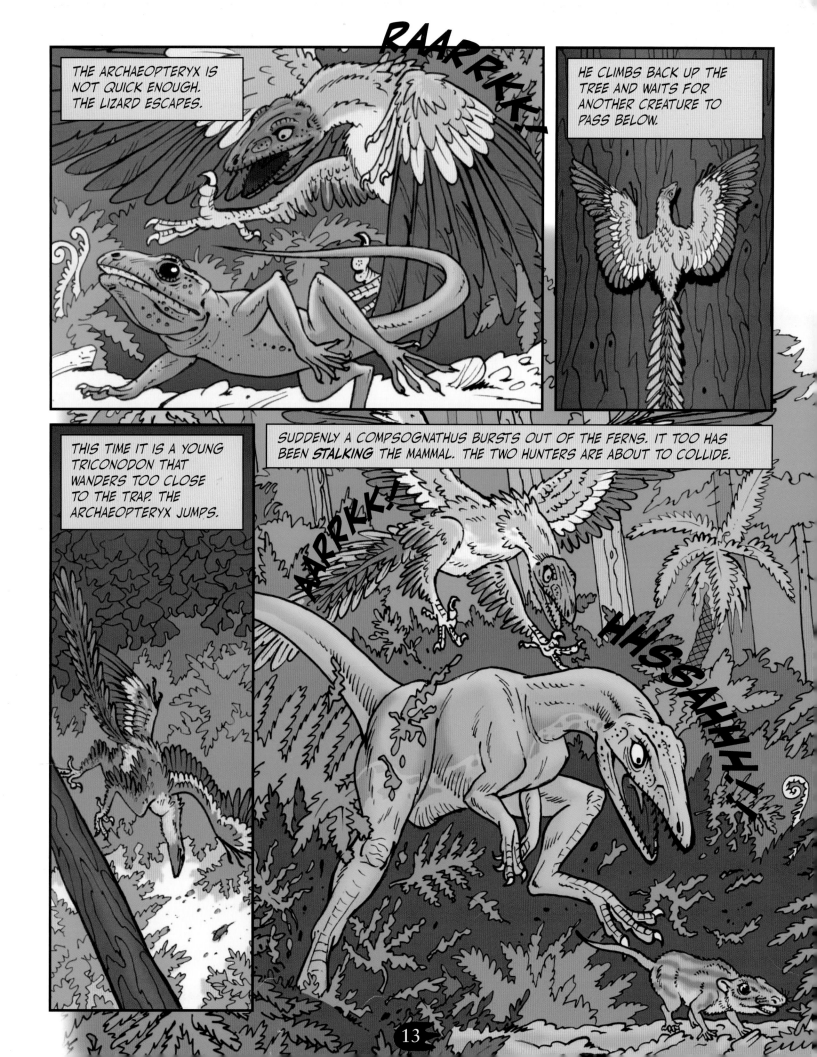

THE ARCHAEOPTERYX IS NOT QUICK ENOUGH. THE LIZARD ESCAPES.

RAARRKK!

HE CLIMBS BACK UP THE TREE AND WAITS FOR ANOTHER CREATURE TO PASS BELOW.

THIS TIME IT IS A YOUNG TRICONODON THAT WANDERS TOO CLOSE TO THE TRAP. THE ARCHAEOPTERYX JUMPS.

SUDDENLY A COMPSOGNATHUS BURSTS OUT OF THE FERNS. IT TOO HAS BEEN **STALKING** THE MAMMAL. THE TWO HUNTERS ARE ABOUT TO COLLIDE.

AARRKK!

HHSSAHHH!

IT LOOKS AS IF THEY WILL CRASH, BUT AT THE LAST SECOND THE ARCHAEOPTERYX SPREADS HIS WINGS AS FAR AS HE CAN. HE STOPS FALLING AND SWOOPS OVER THE DINOSAUR'S SNAPPING JAWS.

HE CONTINUES TO RISE, SOARING ABOVE THE FERNS.

FOR THE FIRST TIME, THE ARCHAEOPTERYX IS FLYING.

RRAARRHHHGHH!!

AS THE ARCHAEOPTERYX SLOWS DOWN, HE BEGINS TO FALL...

BOOUFF...

...AND LANDS WITH A BUMP.

BEFORE LONG HIS FLIGHT FEATHERS HAVE COMPLETELY GROWN IN. THE ARCHAEOPTERYX CANNOT FLY LIKE A MODERN-DAY BIRD, BUT GLIDES FROM TREE TO TREE. IT IS ENOUGH TO KEEP HIM OUT OF DANGER, AND TO HELP HIM SPOT A MEAL.

PART THREE... ISLAND LIFE

IT IS DAWN IN THE FOREST. WHILE THE COOL NIGHT HAS LEFT MANY ANIMALS SLOW AND SLEEPY, ARCHAEOPTERYX'S FEATHERS HAVE KEPT HIM WARM. HE IS WIDE AWAKE AND IS HUNTING FOR HIS BREAKFAST.

THE ARCHAEOPTERYX IS TWO YEARS OLD AND IS A GOOD FLIER. HE SEES A DRAGONFLY ON A FERN. THE SUN HAS NOT WARMED IT YET, AND IT IS DROWSY. THE ARCHAEOPTERYX LEAPS FROM HIS PERCH. THE INSECT TRIES TO ESCAPE, BUT IT IS TOO SLOW.

THE ARCHAEOPTERYX SNAPS THE DRAGONFLY UP IN ITS JAWS...

...AND LANDS ON A TREE TRUNK TO FEED.

THE TREE IS HOME TO A FLOCK OF NESTING ANUROGNATHUSES. THESE TINY FLYING REPTILES SEE THE ARCHAEOPTERYX AS A THREAT TO THEIR EGGS AND NESTLINGS.

THE ANUROGNATHUSES TAKE TO THE AIR. THEY WILL TRY TO CHASE HIM AWAY.

THE ARCHAEOPTERYX GLIDES FROM THE TREE WITH THE FLYING REPTILES CLOSE BEHIND. THEY SPIN AND WHIRL AROUND THE FLEEING INTRUDER. THE ARCHAEOPTERYX IS FORCED TO DROP HIS DRAGONFLY.

THE ANUROGNATHUSES FORGET THE CHASE AND SWOOP AFTER THE INSECT.

AACHK!!

AACHK!!

AACHK!!

AACHK!!

AACHK!!

AS THE ANUROGNATHUSES FLY BACK TO THEIR NESTLINGS, THE ARCHAEOPTERYX LANDS ON THE FOREST FLOOR. HE IS STILL HUNGRY.

A FAMILY OF EUROPASAURUSES WALKS THROUGH THE DENSE BRACKEN.

THE EUROPASAURUSES ARE LONG-NECKED DINOSAURS, BUT THEY ARE MUCH SMALLER THAN THEIR GIANT COUSINS ON THE MAINLAND.

THERE ARE NO LARGE PREDATORS ON THE ISLAND, SO THEY HAVE NOT HAD TO BECOME LARGE THEMSELVES TO SURVIVE.

THE ARCHAEOPTERYX FOLLOWS THE EUROPASAURUSES.

HE IS HOPING TO CATCH ANY INSECTS OR LIZARDS THEY MIGHT DISTURB.

BUT HE IS OUT OF LUCK. HE CLIMBS A TREE IN SEARCH OF GRUBS HIDDEN IN ITS BARK.

ABOVE HIM A FLOCK OF GERMANODACTYLS ARE HEADING TO THE SEA. HE MAY HAVE MORE SUCCESS THERE, HUNTING AMONG THE SAND DUNES.

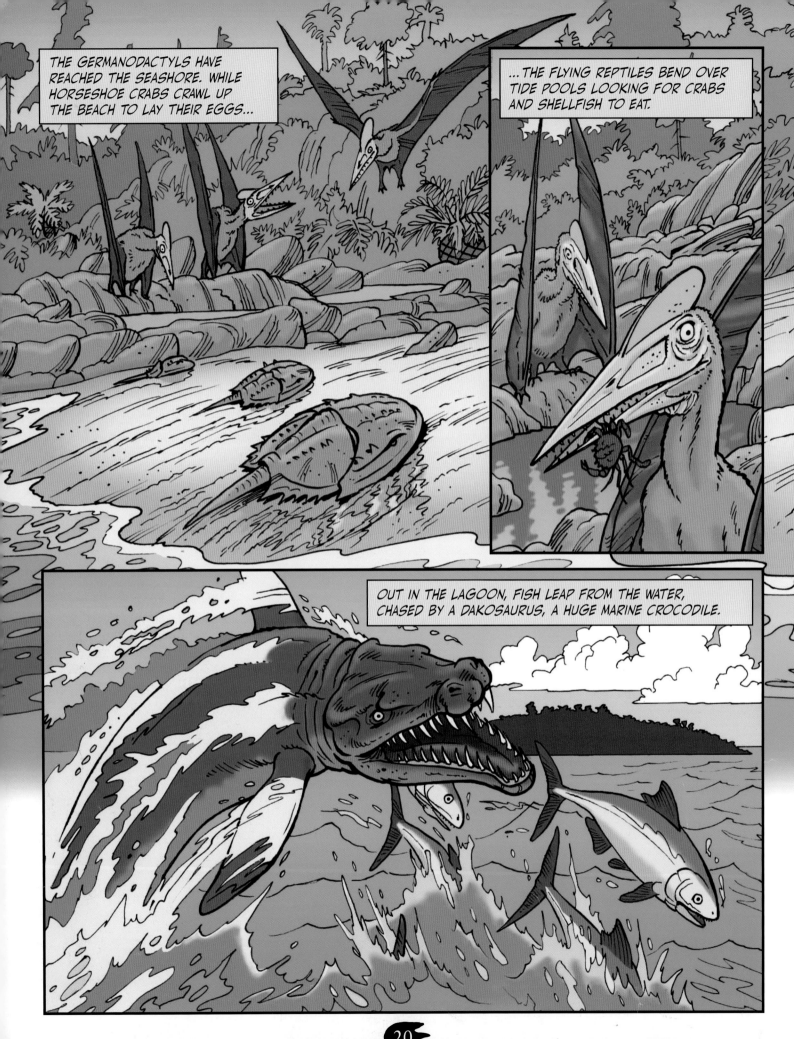

THE GERMANODACTYLS HAVE REACHED THE SEASHORE. WHILE HORSESHOE CRABS CRAWL UP THE BEACH TO LAY THEIR EGGS...

...THE FLYING REPTILES BEND OVER TIDE POOLS LOOKING FOR CRABS AND SHELLFISH TO EAT.

OUT IN THE LAGOON, FISH LEAP FROM THE WATER, CHASED BY A DAKOSAURUS, A HUGE MARINE CROCODILE.

THE ARCHAEOPTERYX HAS FOLLOWED THE GERMANODACTYLS TO THE SEA. HE SOON SPOTS A SMALL LIZARD BASKING IN THE DUNES AND CHASES AFTER IT.

A SOUND CATCHES HIS ATTENTION. HE FORGETS THE LIZARD AND GOES TO SEE WHAT THE NOISE IS.

STRANGE SOUNDS ARE COMING FROM BENEATH THE SAND.

RRARRK!
RRARRKA
RRARRK!
RRARRK!

THE ARCHAEOPTERYX BEGINS TO DIG.

THE SOUNDS ARE COMING FROM A CLUTCH OF EGGS BURIED IN THE WARM SAND. THEY WILL MAKE A TASTY MEAL FOR THE HUNGRY ARCHAEOPTERYX.

RRARRK!

RRARRK!

RRARRK!

A COMPSOGNATHUS HAS ALSO BEEN DRAWN THERE BY THE UNUSUAL NOISES.

COMPSOGNATHUSES ARE SMALL, BUT ON THIS ISLAND THEY ARE THE LARGEST LAND PREDATOR. THE NEWCOMER EASILY DRIVES THE ARCHAEOPTERYX FROM THE NEST.

THE ARCHAEOPTERYX CLIMBS TO SAFETY IN THE NEAREST TREE FERN.

SSZHHAARGH!!

WAARRK!!

MEANWHILE, THE SOUNDS FROM THE EGGS HAVE GROWN LOUDER. THEY START TO HATCH.

THEY ARE STENEOSAURUS HATCHLINGS. THE YOUNG CROCODILES WERE CALLING TO THEIR MOTHER WHILE THEY WERE STILL INSIDE THEIR EGGS. SHE HAS HEARD THEM AND HAS COME TO PROTECT THEM.

RRARRK!

RRARRK!

ROUARRR!!

HSSHAAHH!!

RRARRK!

RRARRK!

RRARRK!

THE COMPSOGNATHUS IS NO MATCH FOR THE STENEOSAURUS. THE ARCHAEOPTERYX WATCHES AS THE DINOSAUR IS DRIVEN AWAY BY THE ANGRY SEA CROCODILE.

THE ARCHAEOPTERYX IS ALL ALONE. HE HAS HAD ENOUGH OF THE SEA AND WANTS TO GO HOME. HE SEES A TREE FERN AND LEAPS TOWARD IT. THE FOREST IS A LONG WAY OFF, AND HE IS STILL HUNGRY.

PART FOUR... MAKING FRIENDS

IT IS SIX MONTHS LATER. THE ARCHAEOPTERYX IS NEARLY THREE YEARS OLD AND IS NOW FULL-GROWN. HIS OLD FEATHERS HAVE BEEN **SHED** AND NEW, BRIGHTLY COLORED ONES HAVE GROWN IN THEIR PLACE. THEY HAVE KEPT HIM WARM AND DRY DURING THE SHORT WET SEASON.

THE RAIN HAS STOPPED. THE ARCHAEOPTERYX SHAKES HIS FEATHERS DRY, **PREENS** THEM...

...AND FLIES OFF IN SEARCH OF A MEAL.

HE ENTERS A CLEARING.

THERE, SITTING ON THE BRANCH OF A TREE, IS ANOTHER ARCHAEOPTERYX.

IT IS A YOUNG FEMALE.

HE FORGETS ABOUT FOOD. HERE IS A CHANCE TO WIN A MATE. HE CALLS OUT.

WAAWAARRK!!.

THE FEMALE IGNORES HIM AND FLIES DEEPER INTO THE FOREST.

THE ARCHAEOPTERYX FOLLOWS.

BUT THE FEMALE FLIES OFF WHENEVER HE GETS NEAR.

FINALLY THE ARCHAEOPTERYX MANAGES TO GET CLOSE TO THE FEMALE. HE TRIES TO IMPRESS HER WITH HIS BRIGHT NEW **PLUMAGE**.

BUCKK!
KK!

HE NEEDS TO LOOK AS HEALTHY AND STRONG AS POSSIBLE. THE FEMALE MUST THINK HE WILL MAKE A GOOD PARTNER.

THE DISPLAY DOES NOT SEEM TO INTEREST HER, THOUGH. A SUDDEN CRY CAUSES THE ARCHAEOPTERYX TO STOP AND TURN AROUND.

A SECOND MALE ARCHAEOPTERYX SITS IN A NEARBY TREE. HE TOO HAS BEEN DRAWN THERE BY THE FEMALE. THE NEWCOMER LETS OUT ANOTHER HARSH SQUAWK. IT IS A CHALLENGE TO FIGHT.

WARRCCKK!!

THE TWO MALES FLY DOWN TO THE FOREST FLOOR AND CIRCLE EACH OTHER.

THEY SCREAM AND SCREECH, AND PUFF OUT THEIR FEATHERS TO MAKE THEMSELVES LOOK AS BIG AS THEY CAN. NEITHER ANIMAL WILL BACK DOWN.

ARRARRACCKK!!

ARRARRCCKK!!

WITHOUT WARNING, THE TWO BIRDS FLY AT EACH OTHER, STRIKING AGAIN AND AGAIN WITH THEIR KILLING CLAWS.

MEANWHILE, THE FEMALE WATCHES THE FIGHT FROM HER TREE.

THE FIGHT ENDS AS QUICKLY AS IT BEGAN. THE NEWCOMER HAS LOST AND IS CHASED AWAY

WAARRCKK!!

THE WINNER REMEMBERS THE FEMALE AND RETURNS TO THE SCENE OF THE FIGHT. HE IS ALONE. THE FEMALE IS GONE.

HE CALLS...

WAAWAARRCKK!!

...AND HEARS A REPLY. IT IS THE MISSING FEMALE.

AARRCKK!!

SHE IS WAITING IN A TREE NEARBY. THE MALE JOINS HER. THIS TIME SHE DOES NOT FLY AWAY.

UCKK! UCKK!

FOSSIL EVIDENCE

SCIENTISTS LEARN WHAT DINOSAURS MAY HAVE LOOKED LIKE BY STUDYING THEIR FOSSIL REMAINS. FOSSILS ARE FORMED WHEN THE HARD PARTS OF AN ANIMAL OR PLANT ARE BURIED AND TURN TO ROCK OVER THOUSANDS OF YEARS.

In 1860, a fossilized feather was found in a limestone quarry near Solnhofen, Germany. The following year a fossilized skeleton was unearthed in the same quarry. It seemed to be a small meat-eating dinosaur, but the outline of feathers could be seen along its tail, and it had feathered wings. At that time scientists thought that only birds had wings and feathers, so it was grouped with the bird family and named Archaeopteryx, or "ancient wing," because it was 100 million years older than the oldest known bird. Since then nine other Archaeopteryx fossils have been found, all in the same part of Germany. Scientists now know that some nonflying dinosaurs had feathers too, but the feathers from Archaeopteryx's wings were the right shape for it to fly.

The fossil feather (above) that was discovered in 1860 was thought to belong to an Archaeopteryx.

Feathers on the wings and tail (right) can be seen on this fossil Archaeopteryx.

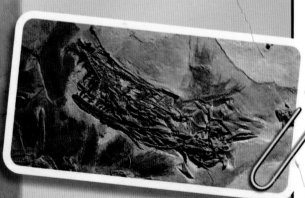

A fossil skull of the dinosaur Sinornithosaurus (above), shows its downy feathers.

ANIMAL GALLERY

ALL THESE ANIMALS APPEAR IN THE STORY.

Bavarisaurus
"Bavarian lizard"
Length: 12 in
(30 cm)
A small extinct lizard
related to the
modern-
day
monitor lizard.

Triconodon
"Three-spiked tooth"
Length: 12 in (30 cm)
A small extinct
mammal that ate
insects.

Anurognathus
"Tailless jaw"
Wingspan: 20 in
(50 cm)
A flying reptile that
was 3.5 in (9 cm) long.

Juravenator
"Hunter from the
Jura Mountains"
Length: 28 in (70 cm)
A meat-eating
dinosaur that may
have had feathers.

Germanodactylus
"German finger"
Wingspan: 39 in (1 m)
A medium-sized, crested flying
reptile that ate shellfish.

Compsognathus
"Elegant jaw"
Length: 39 in (1 m)
The meat-eating
Compsognathus was once the
smallest known dinosaur.

Steneosaurus
"Narrow lizard"
Length: 5 ft (1.5 m)
A small saltwater crocodile that
used its long snout to
catch fish.

Dakosaurus
"Tearing lizard"
Length: 16 ft (5 m)
A large meat-eating marine
crocodile that spent all its life
at sea.

Europasaurus
"European lizard"
Length: 20 ft (6 m)
A plant-eating, long-necked
dinosaur that was much
smaller than others of its kind.

Camptosaurus
"Bent lizard"
Length: 26 ft (8 m)
A large, beaked dinosaur that
used its hundreds of teeth to
chew tough vegetation.

GLOSSARY

clamber (KLAM-burr) To climb in, up, or out of something.

evolved (ih-VOLVD) Changed from one thing into something else.

fossils (FO-sulz) The remains of living things that have turned to rock.

intruder (in-TROOD-er) Someone or something that enters uninvited.

Jurassic period (juh-RAS-sik PIR-ee-ud) The time between 208 and 146 million years ago.

plumage (PLOO-mij) A bird's feathered coat.

preens (PREENZ) Cleans and straightens feathers.

shed (SHED) To lose hair, feathers, or skin.

stalking (STOK-ing) Secretly following someone or something.

INDEX

Web Sites
Due to the changing nature of Internet links, the Rosen Publishing Group, Inc., has developed an online list of Web sites related to the subject of this book. This site is updated regularly. Please use this link to access the list:
www.powerkidslinks.com/gdino/arch/

2/12